UPDATED EDITION

Guess What!

Student's Book 1A
with eBook

American English

Susannah Reed with Kay Bentley

Series Editor: Lesley Koustaff

CAMBRIDGE

Contents

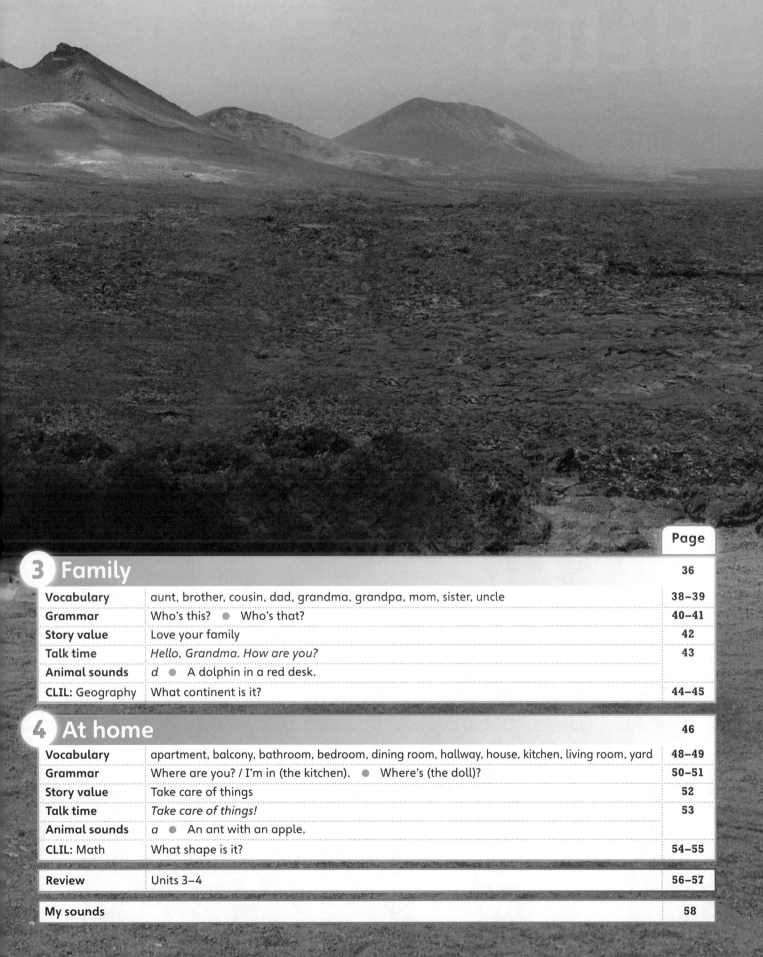

Hello!

Guess What!

5

1 🎧 0.01 **Listen. Who's speaking?**

2 🎧 0.02 **Listen, point, and say.**

3 🎧 0.03 **Listen and find.**

Find Leo

4 **Say the chant.**

5 Think **Look and say the name.**

Number 1. David.

6  **Listen, look, and say.**

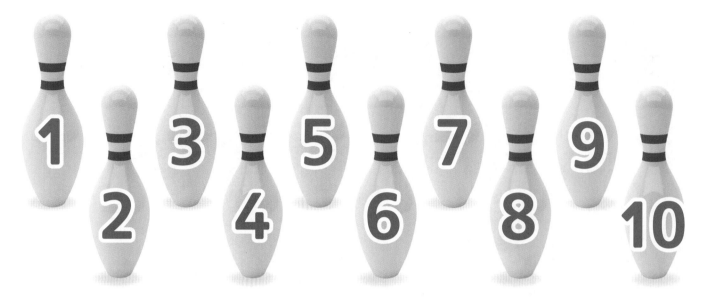

7 **Look and match.**

8 **Now listen and check.**

Grammar: *Numbers 1–10*

→ Workbook page 6

9 **Listen, point, and say.**

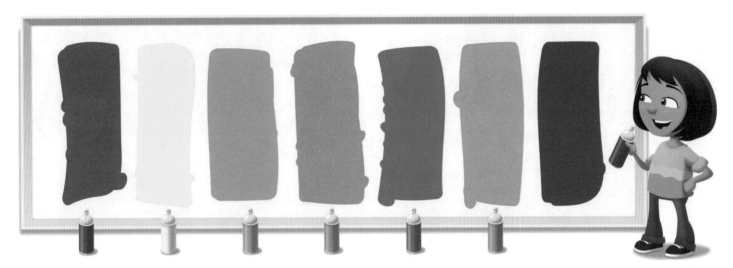

10 **Sing the song.**

11 **Ask and answer.**

How old are you?   I'm six.

What's your favorite color?   My favorite color's blue.

Grammar fun!

1

2

3

4

5

6

Value: Be curious

→ Workbook page 8

13 **Listen and act.**

Animal sounds

14 **Listen and say.**

A pink and purple panda.

→ Workbook page 9   Functional language: *Look! It's a lizard!*   Pronunciation: p. **11**

What color is it?

1 🎧 0.18 **Listen and say.**

2 ▶ CLIL **Watch the video.**

3 **Say the color.**

Number 1. Orange.   Yes.

Guess What!

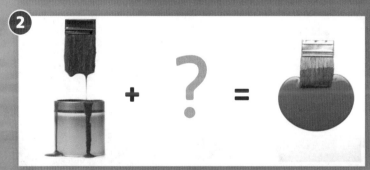

Let's collaborate!

OUR **COLOR COLLAGE**

think find
choose compare
color
create

1 School

Look!

Guess What!

15

1 🎧 1.01 **Listen. Who's speaking?**

2 🎧 1.02 **Listen, point, and say.**

3 🎧 1.03 **Listen and find.**

Find Leo

4 🎧 1.05 **Say the chant.**

 5 Think **Look and find five differences.**

Picture 1. A purple pen.   Picture 2. A purple pencil.

6 🎧 1.07 **Sing the song.**

7 🎧 1.08 **Listen and answer the questions.**

How many chairs can you see?

Six!

Grammar fun!

Grammar: *How many chairs can you see?*
→ Workbook page 14

8 (1.09) **Listen, point, and say.**

9 (1.10) **Listen and do the action.**

10 **Play the game.**

Open your book.

Grammar: *Stand up, please.*

Grammar fun!

19

12 **Talk Time** **Listen and act.**

Animal sounds

13 🎧 1.15 **Listen and say.**

A bear with a blue book.

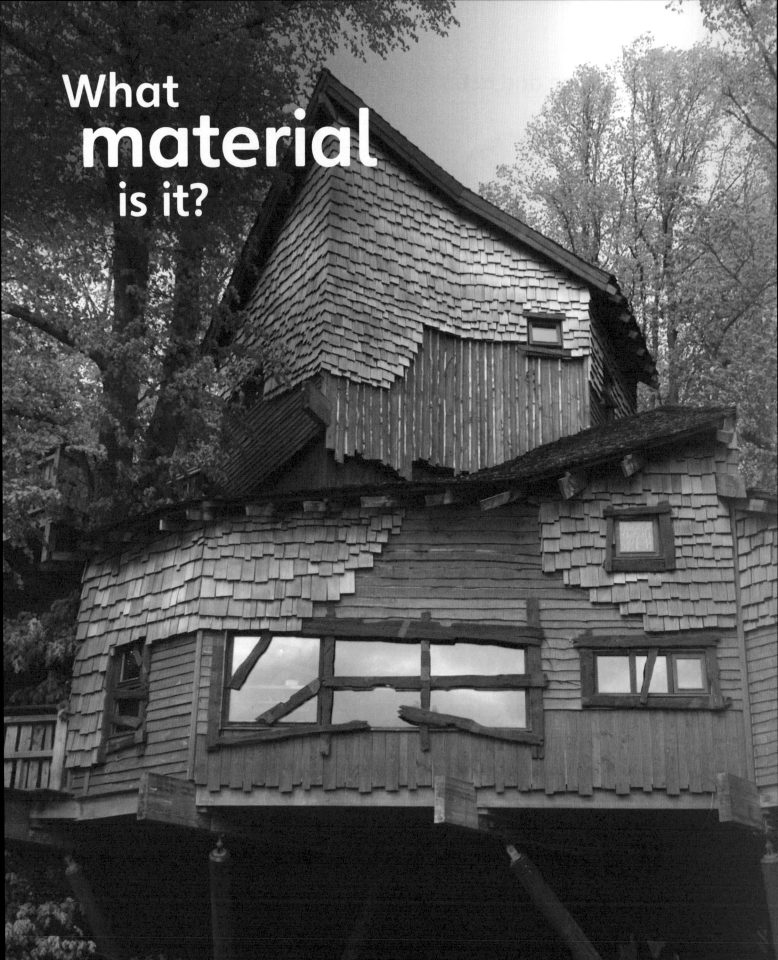

What
material
is it?

1 🎧 1.17 Listen and say.

2 CLIL ▶ Watch the video.

3 Look and say *wood, plastic, metal,* or *glass.*

Number 1. Wood.   Yes.

Guess What!

Let's collaborate!

OUR MATERIALS POSTER

plastic

create

draw

wood   metal   glass

② Toys

Look!

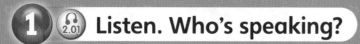

1 🎧 2.01 Listen. Who's speaking?

2 🎧 2.02 Listen, point, and say.

3 🎧 2.03 Listen and find.

Find Leo

Say the chant.

5 (Think) **Look and find five missing toys in picture 2.**

The yellow ball.

→ Workbook page 21

6 🎧 (2.07) **Listen, look, and say.**

1

2

7 (Think) **Look and say.**   What's this?   It's a kite.

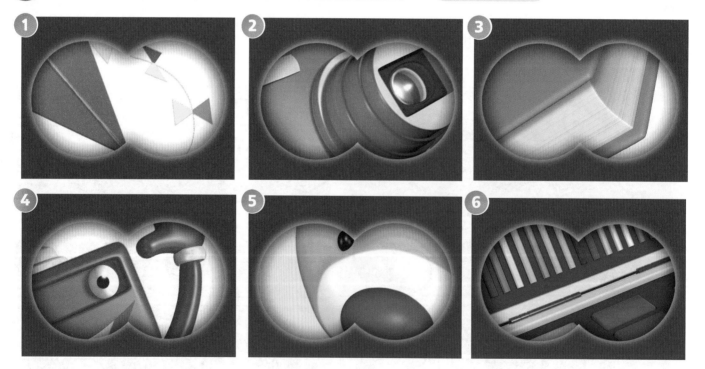

8 🎧 (2.08) **Now listen and check.**

Grammar fun!

Grammar: *What's this?*   → Workbook page 22

9 🎧 2.10 **Sing the song.**

10 **Play the game.**

12 **Talk Time** **Listen and act.**

Animal sounds

13 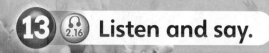 **Listen and say.**

A **turtle** with **two teddy** bears.

Is it electric?

1 🎧 2.18 Listen and say.

1

2

3

2 CLIL ▶ Watch the video.

3 Look and say *it's electric* or *it isn't electric*.

Number 1. It isn't electric.   Yes.

Guess What!

Let's collaborate!

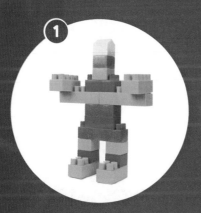

1

2

3

4

OUR BOARD GAME

count

play

colors

1 2 3 4 5 6 7 8 9 0

numbers

questions ?

toys

Review Units 1 and 2

1 Look and say the word. Number 1. Desk.

2 🎧 2.20 Listen and say the color.

→ Workbook pages 28–29

3 **Play the game.**

Blue
What's this?
It's a (pencil case).

Red
Is it a (teddy bear)?
Yes, it is.
Is it an (art set)?
No, it isn't.

Finish

12

11

10

9

8

6

5

7

4

Yellow
How many books can you see?
I can see (six books).

1

2

3

Start

3 Family

Look!

Guess What! theme

1 🎧 3.01 **Listen. Who's speaking?**

2 🎧 3.02 **Listen, point, and say.**

1 grandma **2** grandpa

3 dad **4** mom **5** uncle **6** aunt

7 brother **8** sister **9** cousin

3 🎧 3.03 **Listen and find.**

Find Leo

4 (3.04) **Say the chant.**

5 (3.05) Think **Listen and say *yes* or *no*.** This is my dad. No!

6 (3.07) **Sing the song.**

7 (3.08) Think **Listen and say *yes* or *no*.**

Grammar fun!

Grammar: *Who's this?*

→ Workbook page 32

8 Listen, look, and say.

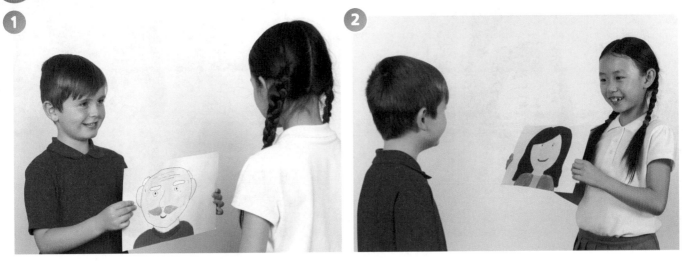

9 Listen and say the color.

10 Draw your family. Ask and answer.

Who's this?

It's my brother. His name's Freddy.

Who's that? Is that your sister?

No, it isn't. It's my cousin.

Grammar: *Who's that?*

Grammar fun!

Value: Love your family

→ Workbook page 34

12   **Listen and act.**

Animal sounds

13 **Listen and say.**

A dolphin in a red desk.

What continent is it?

Ottawa

Madrid

Tokyo

Lima

1 🎧 3.17 Listen and say.

1. North America
2. South America
3. Europe
4. Africa
5. Asia
6. Australia
7. Antarctica

Guess What!

2 CLIL ▶ Watch the video.

3 What continent are they from?

My name's Akiko.
I'm from Tokyo.

My name's Zack.
I'm from Ottawa.

My name's Luiz.
I'm from Lima.

My name's Sofia.
I'm from Madrid.

Let's collaborate!

family   look   discuss   agree   OUR CHILDREN OF THE WORLD BOOKLET   research   continent

4 At home

Guess What!

47

1 🎧 4.01 **Listen. Who's speaking?**

2 🎧 4.02 **Listen, point, and say.**

1 house

2 bathroom

3 bedroom

4 apartment

5 dining room

6 living room

7 balcony

8 kitchen

9 hallway

10 yard

Find Leo

3 🎧 4.03 **Listen and find.**

→ Workbook page 38

4 🎧 4.04 Say the chant.

5 🤔 Think Look and say the room.

Number 1. Dining room.

6 🎧 4.06 **Listen, look, and say.**

7 🎧 4.07 **Listen and say**
Apartment 1 or Apartment 2.

Where's your mom?   Apartment 2.

She's in the bedroom.

Apartment 1

Apartment 2

Grammar fun! ▶   Grammar: *Where are you? / I'm in the kitchen.*   → Workbook page 40

8 (4.08) **Sing the song.**

9 (4.09) **Listen and say *yes* or *no*.**

10 **Ask and answer.**

Where's the doll?

It's under the table.

Yes!

Grammar: *Where's the doll?*

Grammar fun!

🎧 4.11 story ▶ **Listen and watch.**

52   Value: Take care of things

→ Workbook page 42

12 **Talk Time** **Listen and act.**

Animal sounds

13 **Listen and say.**

An ant with an apple.

What shape is it?

1 🎧 4.16 **Listen and say.**

1

circle

2
triangle

3

square

2 CLIL ▶ **Watch the video.**

3 **Look and say** *circle,* *triangle,* **or** *square.*

What's this?   It's a circle!

Guess What!

1

2

3

4

Let's collaborate!

OUR SHAPES PICTURE

think
design
cut
choose
make
share

Review Units 3 and 4

1 Look and say the words. | Number 1. Yard.

2 🎧 4.17 Listen and say the color.

→ Workbook pages 46–47

3 Play the game.

Yellow
Where's the (computer)?
It's (in) the (bedroom).

Orange
Where's your (grandma)?
(She) is in the (bedroom).

Start

Finish

57

My sounds

panda

bear

turtle

dolphin

ant

UPDATED EDITION

Guess What!

Workbook 1A
with Digital Pack

Contents

American English

Susan Rivers

Series Editor: Lesley Koustaff

CAMBRIDGE

Hello!

1 Look and match.

2 Ask and answer with a friend.

1 Hello, I'm Mandy. What's your name?

2 Hello, I'm Jack.

3 This is Penny.

4 Hello, Penny.

3 **Listen and stick.**

4 **Listen and number.**

1

5 🤔 **What's next? Draw a line.**

1. 2 4 6 2 4 6 2 4 ← 10
2. 8 9 10 8 9 10 8 9 → 6
3. 3 5 7 3 5 7 3 5 4
4. 6 5 4 6 5 4 6 5 3
5. 1 8 3 1 8 3 1 8 7

6 🎧 0.09 **Listen and write the numbers in the pictures.**

1.
2.
3.
4.

7  **Listen and color.**

① ② ③

④ ⑤ ⑥

8 (About Me) **Look. Then draw and say.**

① ②

How old are you?

I'm ...

What's your favorite color?

My favorite color's ...

My picture dictionary → Go to page 48: Check the words you know and trace.

9 🎧 0.14 Listen and check ✓.

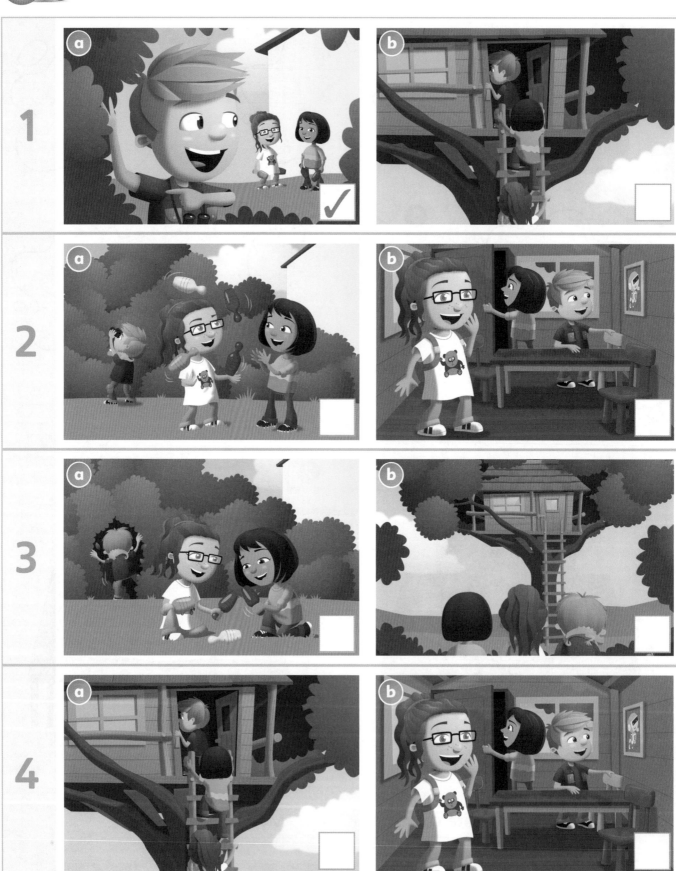

10 **What's missing? Look and draw. Then stick.**

I'm curious.

a
b
c

11 **Trace the letters.**

A pink and purple panda.

12 **Listen and circle the *p* words.**

1

2

3

4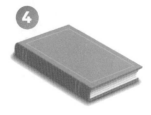

What color is it?

1 🎧 0.19 Listen and color.

2 Look and color.

1  **+**  **=**

2  **+**  **=**

3  **+**  **=**

Evaluation

1 **Follow the lines. Then trace and say.**

a David

b Olivia

c Leo

d Tina

2 **What's your favorite part? Use your stickers.**

story   song   video

3 Puzzle **Trace the color.**

pink

Then go to page 55 and color the Hello! unit pieces.

School

1 🎧 1.04 **Listen and check** ✓.

a [✓]

b [ ]

a [ ]

b abcde [ ]

a [ ]

b [ ]

a [ ]

b [ ]

2 **Look and match.**

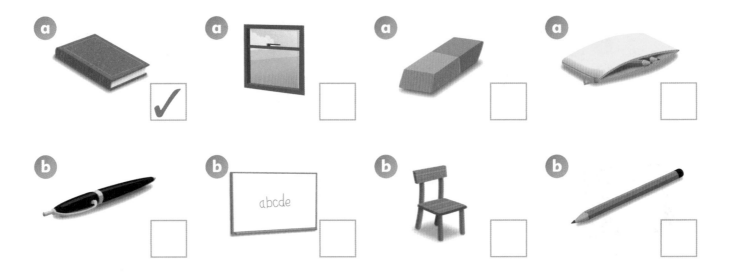

1

2

3

4

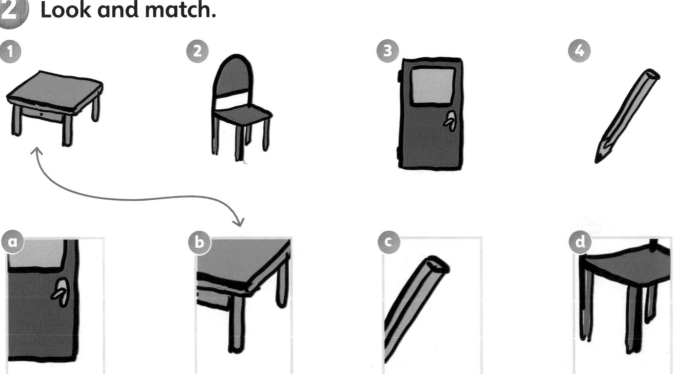

a

b

c

d

3 🎧 1.06 📝 Listen and stick.

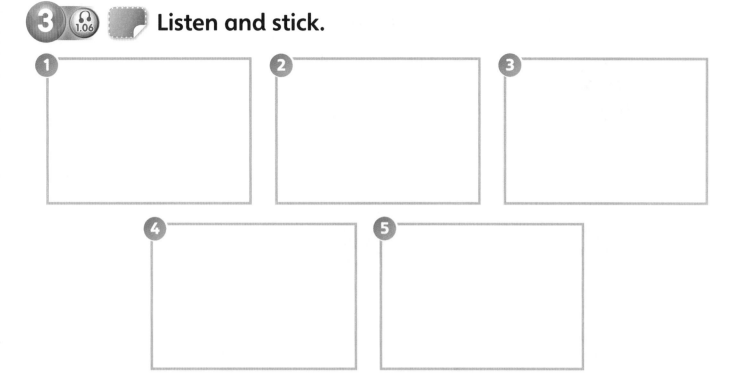

4 Think What's next? Draw a line.

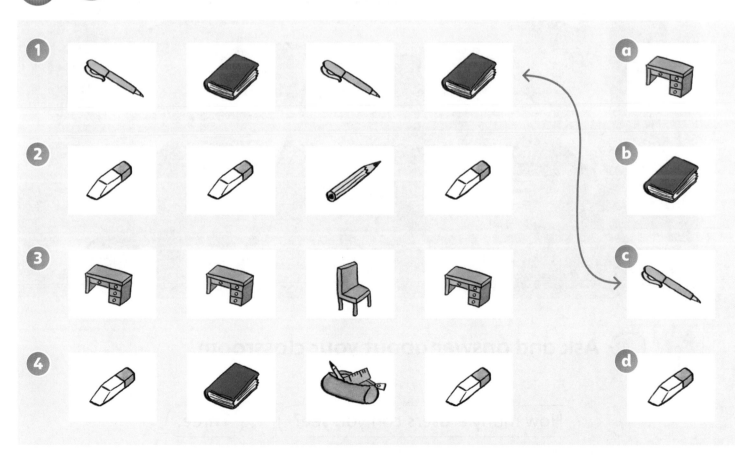

My picture dictionary → Go to page 49: Check the words you know and trace.

5 Look and count. Write the number.

[door] 2	[window] ☐	[desk] ☐
[chair] ☐	[book] ☐	[pencil] ☐

6 Ask and answer about your classroom.

(How many erasers can you see?)   (Three.)

7 🎧 1.11 Listen and check ✓ or put an ✗.

1  ✗

2

3

4

8 Think Circle the different one.

1 a  b  c  d

2 a   b  c   d

Listen, look, and match.

10 **What's missing? Look and draw. Then stick.**

I'm friendly.

a

b

c

11 **Trace the letters.**

A bear with a blue book.

12 **Listen and circle the *b* words.**

1

2

3

4

What **material** is it?

1 Look and match.

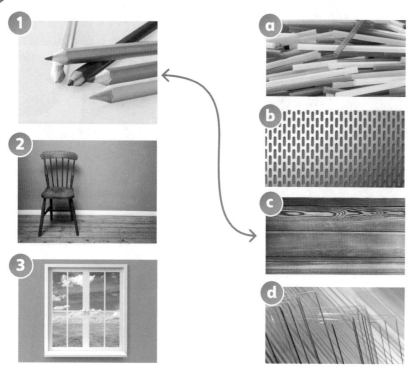

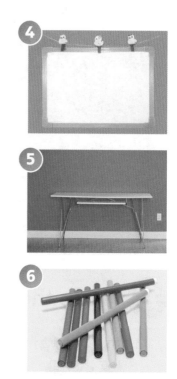

2 Listen and check ✓.

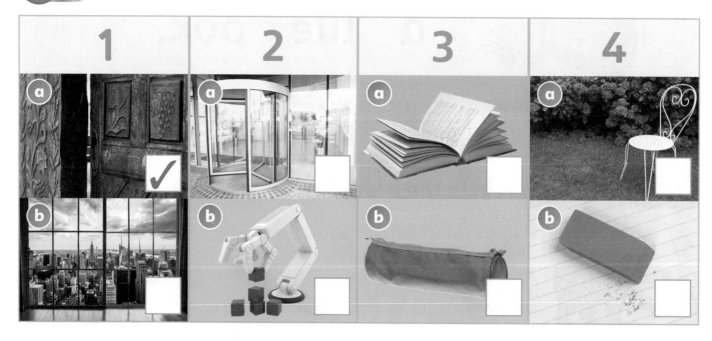

Evaluation

1 **Look and trace. Then say.**

1 book

2 desk

3 pen

4 chair

5 eraser

6 pencil

2 What's your favorite part? Use your stickers.

story   song   video

3 Puzzle **Trace the color.**

red

Then go to page 55 and color the Unit 1 pieces.

2 Toys

1 🎧 (2.04) **Listen and check ✓.**

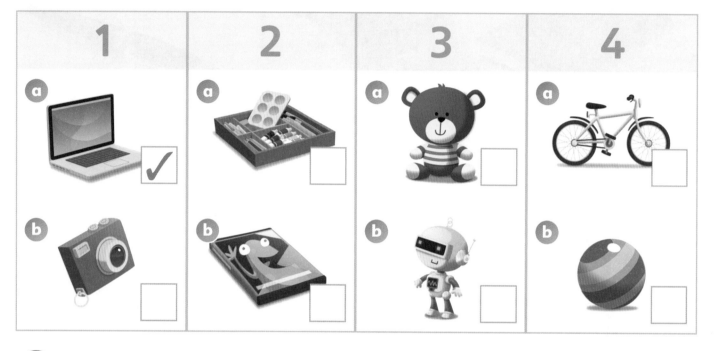

1	2	3	4
a ✓	a	a	a
b	b	b	b

2 **Look, match, and say.** (1 kite.)

3 🎧 2.06 📄 **Listen and stick.**

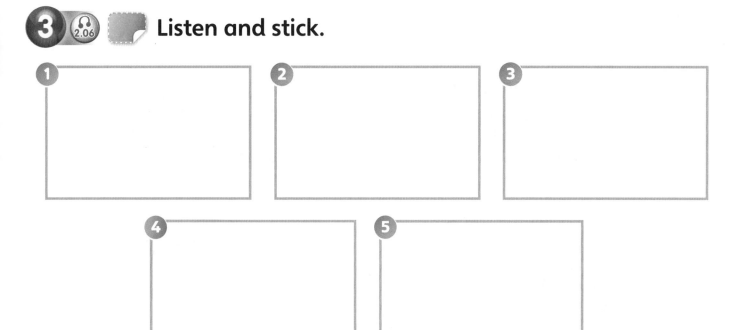

4 Think **Look and circle the toys.**

My picture dictionary Go to page 50: Check the words you know and trace.

5  Listen and check ✔ or put an ✗.

1 ✔

2 ☐

3 ☐

4 ☐

6 (About Me) **Draw your favorite toy and say.**

What's this?

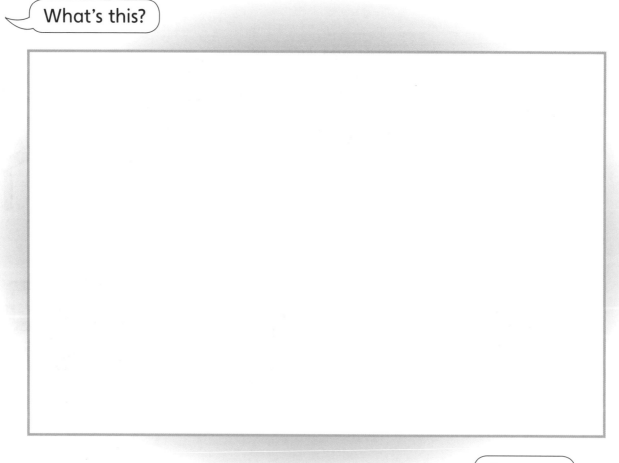

It's a ...

7 🎧 2.11 Listen and number the pictures.

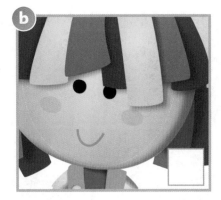

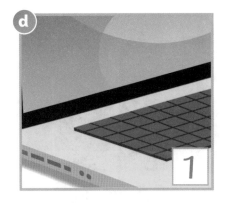

1

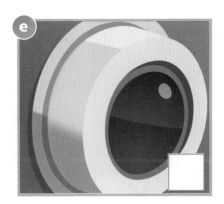

8 🎧 2.12 Listen and draw the pictures.

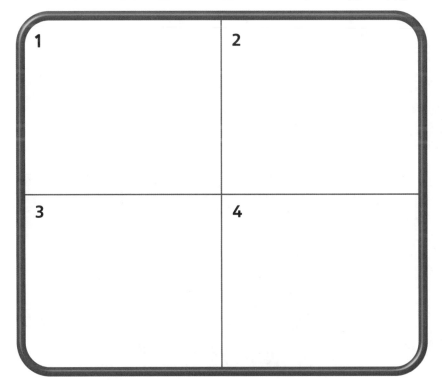

| 1 | 2 |
| 3 | 4 |

9 2.14 Listen and check ✓.

1

a 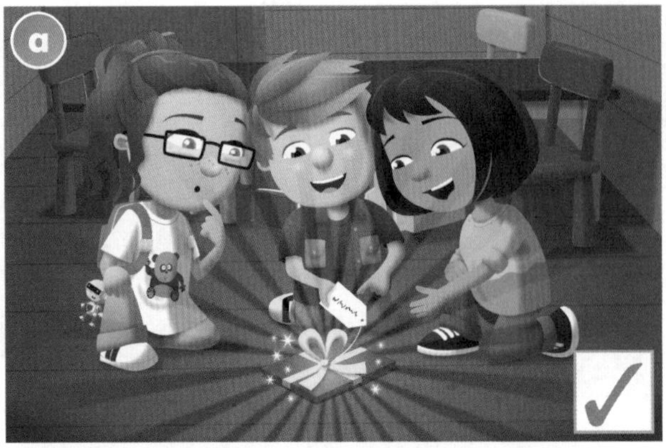 ✓

b 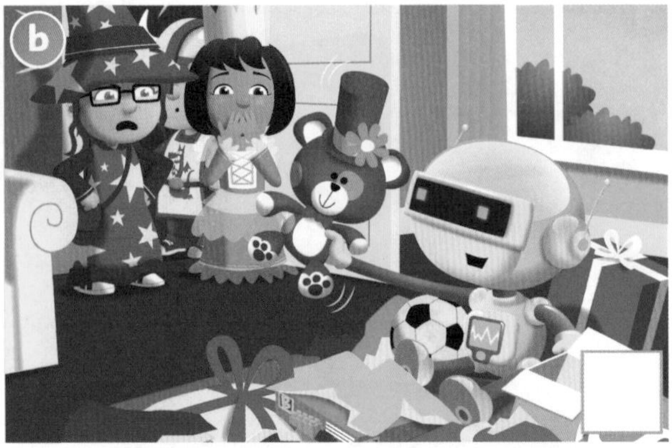

2

a 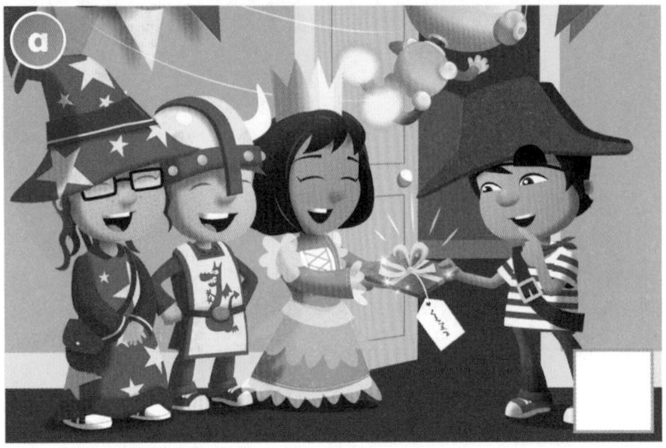

b 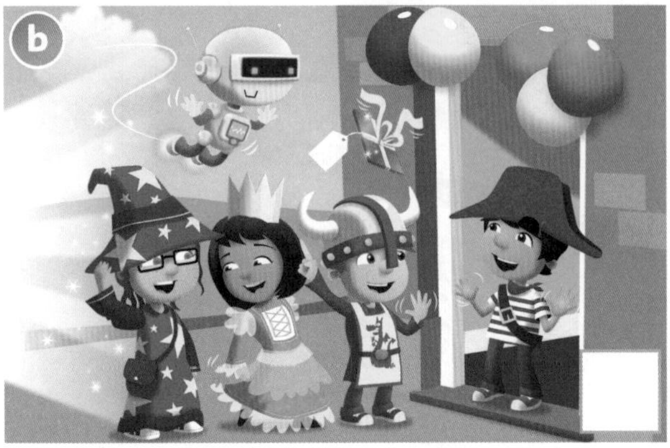

3

a 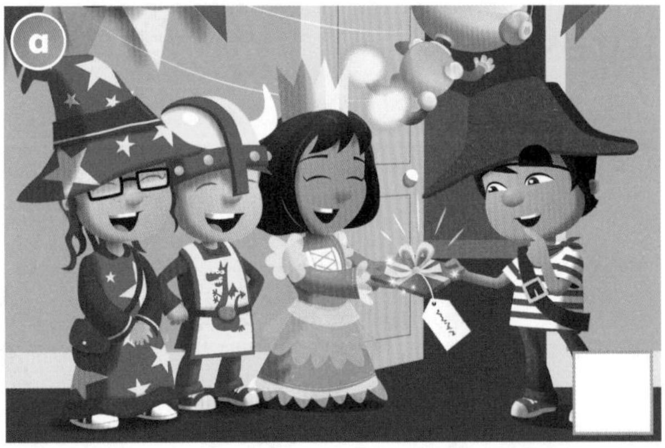

b 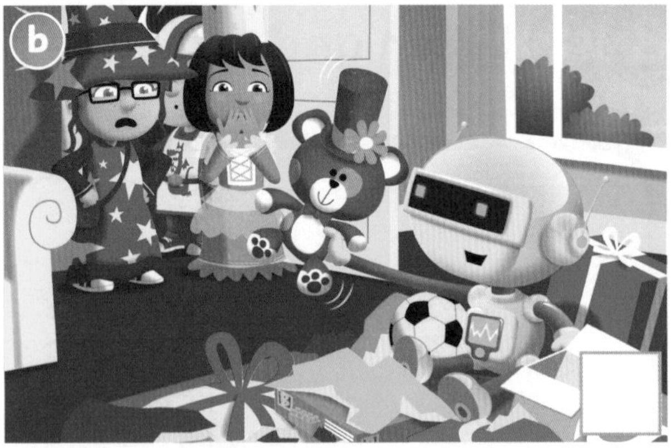

4

a 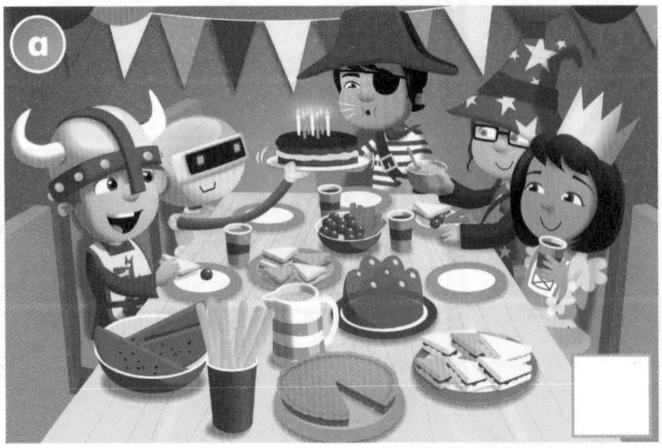

b 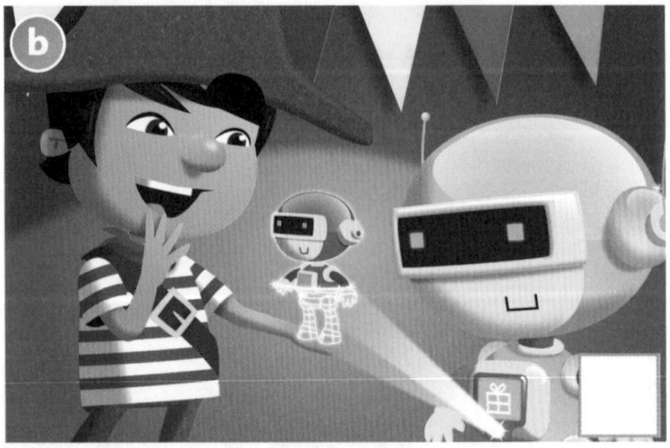

10 **What's missing? Look and draw. Then stick.**

I'm polite.

11 **Trace the letters.**

A turtle with two teddy bears.

12 **Listen and circle the *t* words.**

1
2
3
4

Is it electric?

1 🎧 2.19 **Listen and check ✓ (electric) or put an ✗ (not electric).**

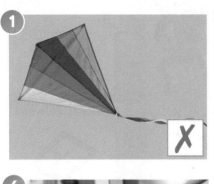 ✗

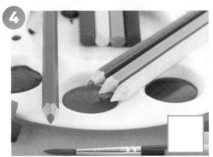

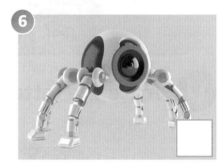

2 **Look at Activity 1 and draw.**

Electric	Not electric
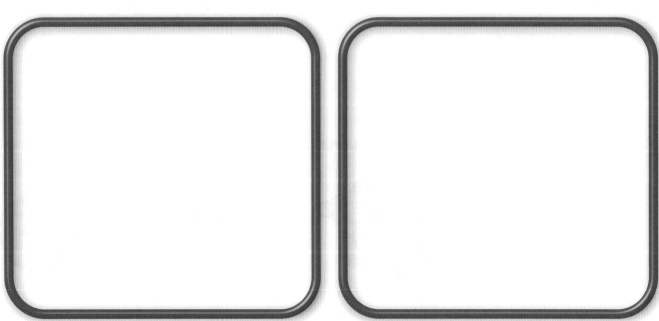	

Evaluation

1 **Look and trace. Then say.**

1
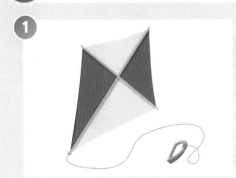
kite

2
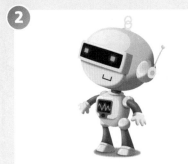
robot

3

ball

4

bike

5

doll

6

camera

2 **What's your favorite part? Use your stickers.**

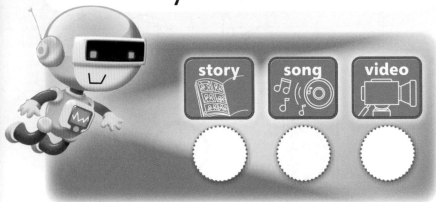

story   song   video

3 **Puzzle** **Trace the color.**

green

Then go to page 55 and color the Unit 2 pieces.

Review Units 1 and 2

1 Look and say. Find and circle.

2 🎧 2.21 Listen and number the pictures.

a

b

c

d

1

e

f

7

1 Trace the words and match.

1 mom

2 dad

3 sister

4 brother

5 grandma

a

b

c

e

d

2 Look and write the number.

| 1 ~~cousin~~ | 2 uncle | 3 grandpa | 4 aunt |

1

3 Listen and stick.

| 1 | 2 | 3 | 4 | 5 |

4 Think Read, look, and check ✓.

1 dad

☐ ☐ ✓

2 aunt

☐ ☐ ☐

3 grandma

☐ ☐ ☐

4 brother

☐ ☐ ☐

My picture dictionary → Go to page 51: Check the words you know and trace.

5 **Look, read, and match.**

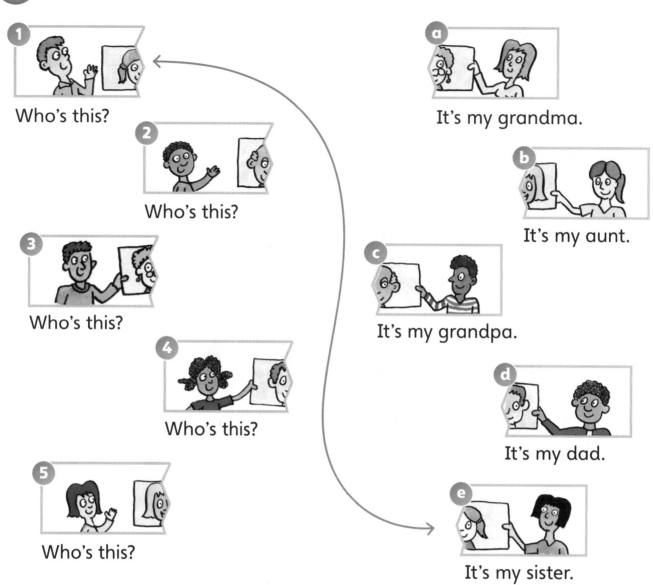

1 Who's this?

2 Who's this?

3 Who's this?

4 Who's this?

5 Who's this?

a It's my grandma.

b It's my aunt.

c It's my grandpa.

d It's my dad.

e It's my sister.

6 (About Me) **Draw a member of your family. Then ask and answer with a friend.**

Who's this?

It's my ...

7 🎧 3.11 **Listen, read, and check ✓.**

1

my brother ☐
my cousin ✓

2

my mom ☐
my aunt ☐

3

my mom ☐
my grandma ☐

4

my sister ☐
my cousin ☐

5

my cousin ☐
my aunt ☐

6

my dad ☐
my uncle ☐

8 **Look, read, and circle the correct word.**

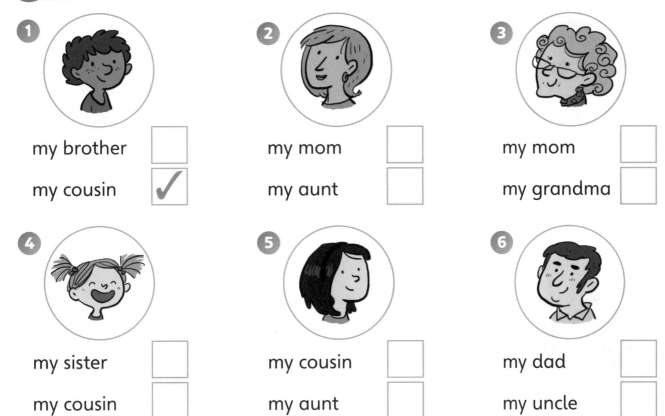

1 Who's **this** / (**that**)?
   It's my uncle.

2 Who's **this** / **that**?
   It's my cousin.

3 Who's **this** / **that**?
   It's my grandpa.

4 Who's **this** / **that**?
   It's my sister.

9 🎧 3.13 **Listen, look, and match.**

10 **What's missing? Look and draw. Then stick.**

I love my family.

11 **Trace the letters.**

A dolphin in a red desk.

12 **(3.16)** **Listen and circle the *d* words.**

1 **2** **3** **4**

What continent is it?

1 🎧 3.18 **Listen and write the number.**

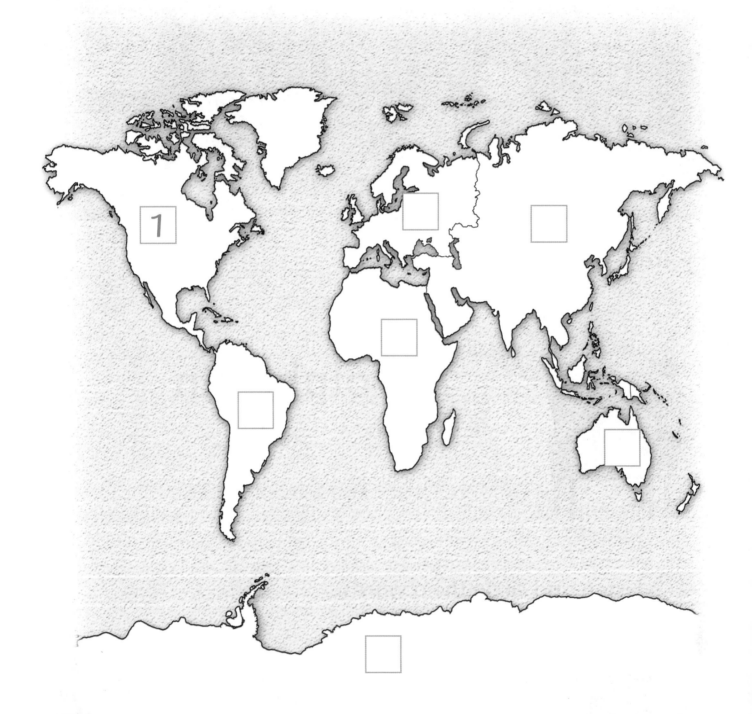

2 🎧 3.19 **Look at the map again. Listen and color.**

Evaluation

1 **Read and trace. Then circle and say.**

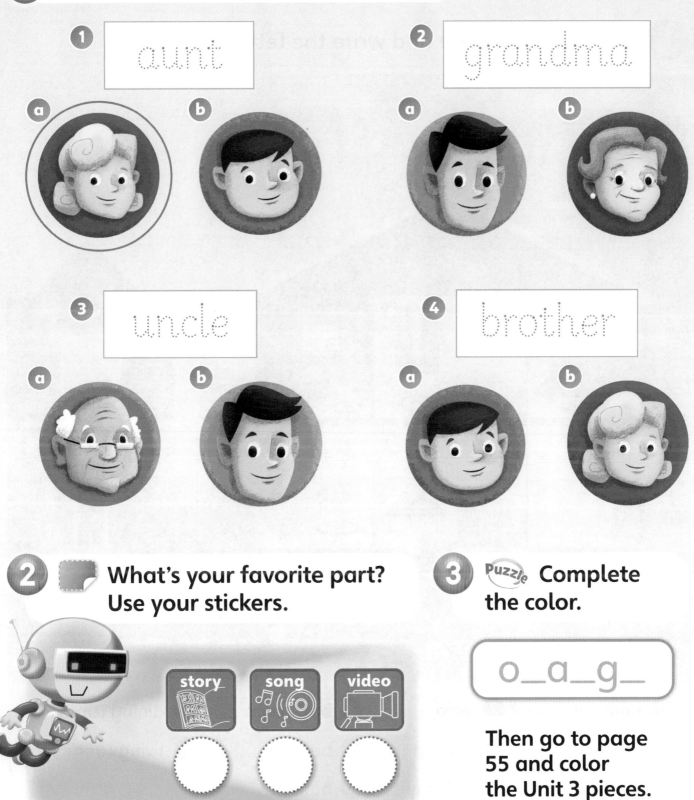

1 aunt
a b

2 grandma
a b

3 uncle
a b

4 brother
a b

2 What's your favorite part? Use your stickers.

story song video

3 Puzzle Complete the color.

o_a_g_

Then go to page 55 and color the Unit 3 pieces.

4 At home

1 Look at the picture and write the letter.

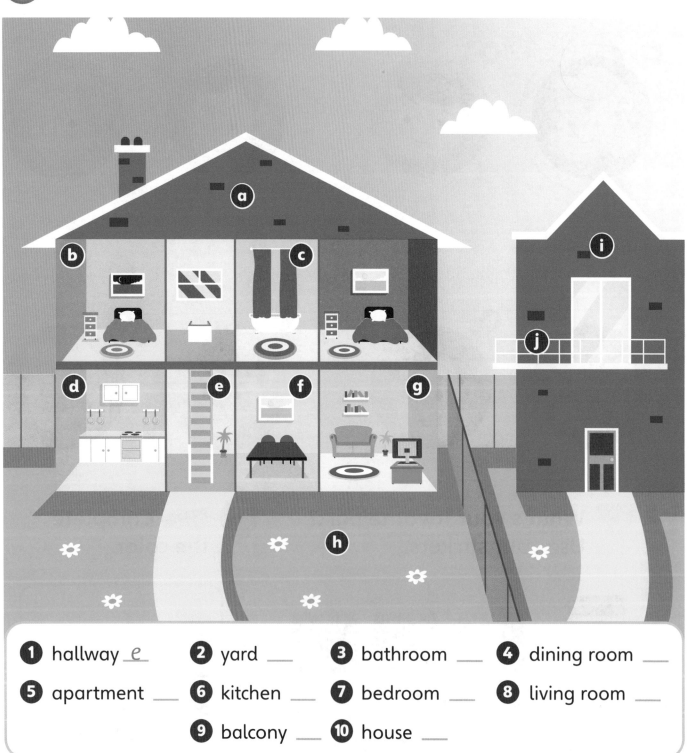

1 hallway _e_ **2** yard ___ **3** bathroom ___ **4** dining room ___

5 apartment ___ **6** kitchen ___ **7** bedroom ___ **8** living room ___

9 balcony ___ **10** house ___

2 **Listen and stick.**

1	2	3

4	5	6

3 **Look, read, and circle the correct word.**

1 (kitchen) / dining room

2 hallway / living room

3 bedroom / balcony

4 kitchen / bathroom

5 hallway / yard

6 balcony / dining room

My picture dictionary ⟶ **Go to page 52: Check the words you know and trace.**

Look, read, and match.

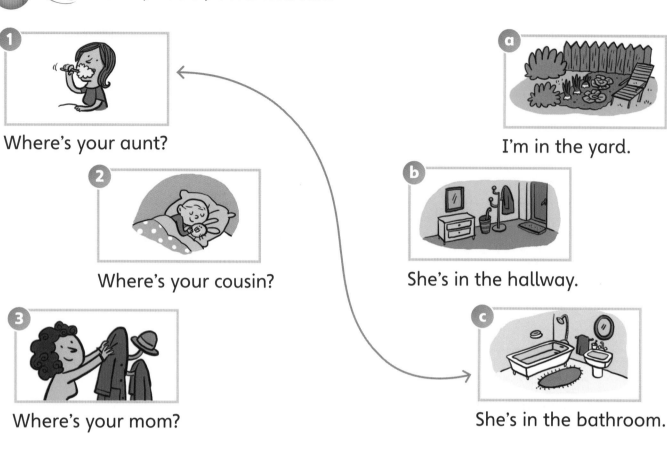

1 Where's your aunt?

2 Where's your cousin?

3 Where's your mom?

4 Where are you?

a I'm in the yard.

b She's in the hallway.

c She's in the bathroom.

d He's in the bedroom.

  Draw yourself. Ask and answer with a friend.

 Where are you?

 I'm in ...

6  **Listen and write the number.**

1 **2**  **3**  **4** 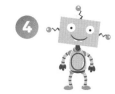 **5**

7 **Draw the objects in the picture. Ask and answer.**

Where's the … ?   It's … .

8 🎧 4.12 Listen and number.

9 **What's missing? Look and draw. Then stick.**

I take care of things.

a

b

c

10 **Trace the letters.**

An ant with an apple.

11 **Listen and circle the *a* words.**

1
2
3
4

What shape is it?

1 Look and color the shapes.

2 What's next? Match, then draw and color the shapes.

square

1 ▲ ● ▲ ● ▲

triangle

2 ■ ■ ● ● ■

circle

3 ● ■ ▲ ● ■

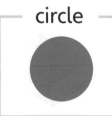

Evaluation

1 Read and trace. Then circle and say.

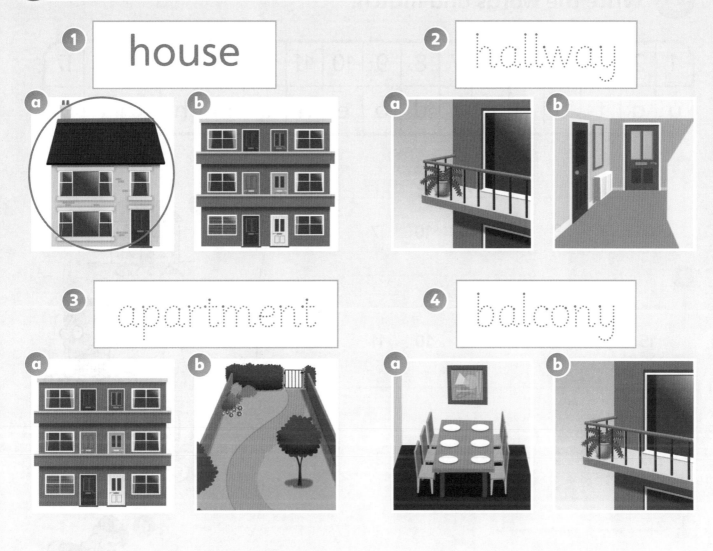

① house

② hallway

③ apartment

④ balcony

2 What's your favorite part? Use your stickers.

story   song   video

3 Puzzle Complete the color.

y_l_o_

Then go to page 55 and color the Unit 4 pieces.

Review Units 3 and 4

1 Write the words and match.

1	2	3	4	5	6	7	8	9	10	11	12	13	14	15	16	17
u	a	t	b	s	c	r	d	o	e	n	g	m	h	k	i	y

1
b r o t h e r
4   7   9   3   14   10   7

2
_ _ _ _ _ _ _
15   16   3   6   14   10   11

3
_ _ _ _ _ _ _
12   7   2   11   8   13   2

4
_ _ _ _
17   2   7   8

5
_ _ _
8   2   8

6
_ _ _ _ _
14   9   1   5   10

a

b

c

d

e

f

2 Read and match the questions with the answers.

1 Where's the computer? _c_
2 Is that your cousin? ___
3 Who's that? ___
4 Where's your mom? ___

a She's in the living room.
b No, it isn't. It's my sister.
c It's on the desk.
d It's my sister.

3 Circle the correct words and write.

mom   bedroom   grandma   ~~under~~

1

What's / (Where's) the doll?

It's _under_ the bed.

2

Who's / Where's this?

It's my _____.

3

Who / Where are you?

I'm in my _____.

4

Is that / Who's your aunt?

No, it isn't.

It's my _____.

Hello!

blue ✓

green ☐

orange ☐

pink ☐

purple ☐

red ☐

yellow ☐

1 School

board ✓

book

chair

desk

door

pen

pencil

pencil case

eraser

window

② Toys

 ✓
art set

 ☐
ball

 ☐
bike

 ☐
camera

 ☐
computer

 ☐
computer game

 ☐
doll

 ☐
kite

 ☐
robot

 ☐
teddy bear

3 Family

aunt ✓

brother ☐

cousin ☐

dad ☐

grandma ☐

grandpa ☐

mom ☐

sister ☐

uncle ☐

4 At home

balcony ✓

bathroom

bedroom

dining room

apartment

yard

hallway

house

kitchen

living room

My puzzle

Acknowledgments

Many thanks to everyone in the excellent team at Cambridge University Press & Assessment in Spain, the UK, and India.

The authors and publishers would like to thank the following contributors:

Blooberry Design: concept design, cover design, book design

Hyphen: publishing management, page make-up

Ann Thomson: art direction

Gareth Boden: commissioned photography

Jon Barlow: commissioned photography

Ian Harker: class audio recording

John Marshall Media: "Grammar fun" recordings

Robert Lee, Dib Dib Dub Studios: song and chant composition

Vince Cross: theme tune composition

James Richardson: arrangement of theme tune

Phaebus: "CLIL" video production

Kiki Foster: "Look!" video production

Bill Smith Group: "Grammar fun" and story animations

Sounds Like Mike Ltd: "Grammar Fun" video production

The authors and publishers acknowledge the following sources of copyright material and are grateful for the permissions granted. While every effort has been made, it has not always been possible to identify the sources of all the material used, or to trace all copyright holders. If any omissions are brought to our notice, we will be happy to include the appropriate acknowledgements on reprinting and in the next update to the digital edition, as applicable.

Key: U = Unit.

Student's Book

Photography

The following photos are sourced from Getty Images:

U0: Fertnig/iStock/Getty Images Plus; szefei/iStock/Getty Images Plus; Mike Kemp/Tetra images; plusphoto/iStock/Getty Images Plus; matty2x4/E+; skodonnell/E+; crossbrain66/E+; cscredon/E+; Weekend Images Inc./E+; BirdImages/E+; PhotoTalk/E+; Apassara Kanha/EyeEm; **U1:** kali9/E+; UltraONEs/iStock/Getty Images Plus; Kimberly Hosey/Moment; MiguelMalo/iStock/Getty Images Plus; Dimitris66/iStock/Getty Images Plus; szefei/iStock/Getty Images Plus; jskiba/E+; hayatikayhan/iStock/Getty Images Plus; Ng Sok Lian/EyeEm; Lucy Lambriex/DigitalVision; Bojan Vlahovic/E+; Natthawut Punyosaeng/EyeEm; Prasert Krainukul/Moment; mirjanajovic/DigitalVision Vectors; SolStock/E+; **U2:** gio_banfi/DigitalVision Vectors; Kutay Tanir/Photodisc; Jupiterimages/Stockbyte; Isabel Pavia/Moment; **U3:** Rick Gomez/Tetra images; Ariel Skelley/DigitalVision; Stockbyte; ViewStock; Tanong Abhivadanasiri/EyeEm; Tetra Images; Floortje/E+; **U4:** Vaughn Greg/Getty Images; Simon Montgomery/Getty Images; Compassionate Eye Foundation/Rob Daly/OJO Images Ltd/DigitalVision; Taiyou Nomachi/DigitalVision; chuckcollier/E+; aliaksei_putau/iStock/Getty Images Plus; Mel Yates/DigitalVision.

The following photos are sourced from other libraries:

U0: Pat Canova/Alamy; Margot Hartford/Alamy; Jose Luis Pelaez Inc/Tetra Images, LLC/Alamy; Leigh Prather/Shutterstock; Jaechang Yoo/TongRo Images/Alamy; Valery Voennyy/Alamy; **U1:** Joshua Davenport/Shutterstock; pics five/Shutterstock; City Living/Alamy; My Life Graphic/Shutterstock; Vorobyeva/Shutterstock; Jesus Keller/Shutterstock; Foonia/Shutterstock; ETIENjones/Shutterstock; sirtravelalot/Shutterstock; **U2:** stable/Shutterstock; Chesky/Shutterstock; Fabrice Lerouge/ONOKY - Photononstop/Alamy; Jolanta Wojcicka/Shutterstock; Andriy Rabchun/Shutterstock; ffolas/Shutterstock; prapann/Shutterstock; mekcar/Shutterstock; Sergiy Kuzmin/Shutterstock; Ociacia/Shutterstock; HomeStudio/Shutterstock; Chiyacat/Shutterstock; archideaphoto/Shutterstock; pics five/Shutterstock; IB Photography/Shutterstock; sunsetman/Shutterstock; Jojje/Shutterstock; Lim Yong Hian/Shutterstock; Craig Jewell/Shutterstock; S-F/Shutterstock; Tetra Images/SuperStock; Stockbroker/MBI/Alamy; AsiaPix/SuperStock; **U3:** Hemis/Alamy; Ariel Skelley/Tetra Images, LLC/Alamy; Classic Collection/Shotshop GmbH/Alamy; Monkey Business Images/Shutterstock; Jolanta Wojcicka/Shutterstock; Ekkaruk Dongpuyow/Alamy; mamahoohooba/Alamy; Bill Miles/Cultura RM/Alamy; Keith Levit/Alamy; **U4:** Radius Images/Design Pics/Alamy; romakoma/Shutterstock; RDFlemming/Shutterstock; Khoroshunova Olga/Shutterstock; Andrew Holt/Alamy; Classic Collection/Shotshop GmbH/Alamy; Breadmaker/Shutterstock; Aardvark/Alamy; Westend61/Westend61 GmbH/Alamy; Flashon Studio/Shutterstock; Stockbroker/MBI/Alamy; Richard Newton/Alamy.

Workbook

Photography

The following photos are sourced from Getty Images:

U0: Franz Wogerer/imageBROKER; UltraONEs/iStock/Getty Images Plus; **U1:** kali9/E+; pixsfile/iStock/Getty Images Plus; Julian Ward/ Moment; Peshkova/iStock/Getty Images Plus; myibean/iStock/ Getty Images Plus; ULTRA.F/Photodisc; sorendls/E+; Spiderstock/ E+; Zoonar RF/Zoonar/Getty Images Plus; Martin Barraud/OJO Images; Bedrin-Alexander/iStock/Getty Images Plus; **U2:** SolStock/ E+; ElementalImaging/E+; longoria-td/iStock/Getty Images Plus; adventtr/E+; peangdao/iStock/Getty Images Plus; LisaValder/E+; Talaj/ iStock/Getty Images Plus; **U4:** Vaughn Greg/Getty Images.

The following photos are sourced from other libraries:

U0: Pat Canova/Alamy; **U1:** City Living/Alamy; BonkersAboutPictures/ Alamy; Nokz/Shutterstock; Bencemor/Shutterstock; stockelements/ Shutterstock; Robert Babczynski/Shutterstock; Potapovpaladin/ Shutterstock; Greens and Blues/Shutterstock; photastic/Shutterstock; **U2:** Andriy Rabchun/Shutterstock; **U3:** Hemis/Alamy; Ekkaruk Dongpuyow/Alamy; **U4:** romakoma/Shutterstock.

Front Cover Photography by Dimitri Otis/Stone/Getty Images.

Illustrations

Aphik; Bill Bolton; Chris Jevons (Bright Agency); Joelle Dreidemy (Bright Agency); Kirsten Collier (Bright Agency); Marcus Cutler (Sylvie Poggio); Marek Jagucki; Mark Duffin; Richard Watson (Bright Agency); Woody Fox (Bright Agency); Graham Kennedy; Hardinge (Monkey Feet); Sarah Jennings (Bright Agency).

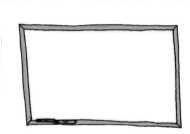

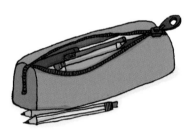